# INSPIRING FABLED SERVICE: PARTICIPANT WORKBOOK

BONNIE JAMESON
BETSY SANDERS

 **Pfeiffer**
& COMPANY
Johannesburg • London
San Diego • Sydney • Toronto

Copyright © 1996 by Pfeiffer & Company
ISBN: 0-88390-473-X

Published by
Pfeiffer & Company
8517 Production Avenue
San Diego, California 92121
United States of America

Editorial Offices: (619) 578-5900, FAX (619) 578-2042
Orders: USA (606) 647-3030, FAX (606) 647-3034

Editor: Marian Prokop
Production Editor: Dawn Kilgore
Interior Design and Page Compositor: Judy Whalen
Cover Design: Lee Ann Hubbard

This book is printed on acid-free, recycled stock that meets or exceeds the
minimum GPO and EPA specifications for recycled paper.

CONTENTS

A Message to the Participant

Companies who are making significant differences in service can be measured by two relevant standards:

♦ Their customers respond with their business; and

♦ Their customers proclaim their excellence.

We call service that is so meaningful to the customers that they care enough about it and are impressed enough to talk about it "fabled service." This is the only level of service that counts with the customer. Thus, it is the only level of service that is worth personal and corporate resources to provide.

A reputation as an excellent service provider has an indisputable impact on the health of a business enterprise. Delighting the customer is the key to fulfilling responsibility to stakeholders of the business. Being known for doing good things for the customers is the most solid basis for long-term success.

Successful service providers share a common understanding of the underlying dynamics of service excellence: Service consists of millions of "Moments of Truth." A moment of truth is any and every encounter your customer has with your company. These include, but are not limited to, front-line people, products, facilities, telephones, billing, advertising, parking lots, packaging, community involvement.... The list is endless and obviously involves every single employee as a service provider.

That there are millions of these moments in which service actually is provided is why the attempt to manage service sometimes seems futile. The book, *Fabled Service: Ordinary Acts, Extraordinary Outcomes*, was written as a handbook for service leaders. Service leadership is neither a title nor a job description. It is merely a commitment on the part of each employee to fully utilize every opportunity to serve the customer. Each chapter in the book includes action steps that provide practice in each element of providing fabled service. These same action steps also appear on the "Commitment" pages in this *Inspiring Fabled Service Participant Workbook*.

The activities you will undertake provide practice in recognizing and maximizing everyday opportunities for service excellence. These opportunities can be summed up quite succinctly, as in has been done by Nordstrom, a fashion specialty store with a reputation for fabled service: Use your own best judgment at all times. And, in every case, is this not what you are going to have to do at the moment of dealing with the customers?

Fabled service providers distinguish themselves in two remarkable ways:

They are the customers. They do not just think like customers, they take the customers to heart and exert every effort to satisfy the customers' needs and solve their problem

They are the company. They have the full resources of the company at their command, and they share responsibility and ownership for the integrity and success of the organization.

In order to reach this optimal level of service performance, people need to have four things:

1. They need to have clear expectations of what they are to accomplish.
   They need to understand the mission.

2. They need to be well-prepared and well-provisioned for their work.
   They need the tools.

3. They need to have barriers removed.
   They need the chance to succeed.

4. They need to have their achievements recognized.
   They need to celebrate and have fun.

These activities are designed to provide you the opportunity to become a fabled service provider. The expectations are clear. The tools are carefully designed. The barriers to your success have been removed. And the time you spend should be truly enjoyable, as you recognize that you have everything within yourself that you need to make yours a fabled service company.

Albert Schweitzer once said, "The only ones among you who will be truly happy are those who have sought and found how to serve." We wish you true happiness as you set out to serve your company, your customers, and your community. Improve even a fraction of those moments of truth, and you will improve the world.

Betsy Sanders
Sutter Creek, California
Bonnie Jameson
Oakland, California

CUSTOMER SERVICE SURVEY

The following three knowledge categories are needed for effective customer service:

1. How well do you know yourself and your leadership role in serving your customer?
2. What do you know about planning for customer service training?
3. What do you know about customer service and product/service knowledge?

Instructions: Read each of the following statements and decide how true it is for you. Choose a response from the following scale and write your answer in the blank that precedes the statement.

Scale:
If the statement is mostly true for you, choose "4."
If the statement is often true for you, choose "3."
If the statement is seldom true for you, choose "2."
If the statement is mostly not true for you, choose "1."

SECTION 1: UNDERSTANDING SELF AND OTHERS

_____I am able to create a climate of trust between my customer and myself.

_____I value my customers and use ethical practices in all of my interactions.

_____I understand psychological type functions and attitudes and can be flexible in my behavior according to my customer's type and temperament.

_____Understanding myself is an important value for me; therefore, I value feedback about myself and my performance.

_____I work to share expectations about our working relationship with my customers.

_____I can handle conflict before it gets out of control.

_____I am able to keep communication channels open through continuing contact with my customers.

_____I can create harmony with supportive and cooperative behavior.

_____I can be assertive without being aggressive or passive.

_____ I am able to be directive and assertive when customers fail to take responsibility.

_____ I am able to influence people in a quiet, personal, and unassuming way.

_____ I can take charge of a situation with command and assurance.

_____ I can set goals, make decisions and give necessary orders.

_____ I am drawn to challenges and new possibilities when serving customers.

_____ I make decisions based on my personal values as well as my logical reasoning.

_____ **Total Score for Section 1**

SECTION 2: STRATEGIC PLANNING FOR RESULTS

_____ I work continually to upgrade my customer service skills.

_____ It is important to understand the needs of customers.

_____ I spend time finding out about my customers and their needs in order to know how I can best serve them.

_____ I develop a personal vision of good customer service for each customer based on his or her needs and expectations.

_____ I understand the internal and external forces that will affect the realization of my vision.

_____ It is important to translate my vision into specific goals in order to satisfy my customers needs.

_____ Each of my goals includes realistic, achievable outcomes.

_____ It is important to develop a time line for achieving my desired outcomes.

_____ My prioritized action plan is an asset in achieving my goals.

_____ I am aware of the resources I need in order to take action.

_____ I am able to delegate action items and roles to the appropriate people.

_____ I plan how I can present my product/service case to meet the needs of my customer.

_____ My plan includes ways to evaluate my customer's satisfaction.

_____ I use evaluation data to continually improve my customer service.

_____ My evaluation summary helps me to set new direction future goals.

_____ **Total Score for Section 2**

Section 3: Product/Service Knowledge

_____ I can clearly and specifically demonstrate my product or service.

_____ I can answer questions from my customers with confidence.

_____ I can respond to customer complaints in a professional manner.

_____ I continually study my product or service to understand how it can benefit my customers.

_____ I help customers identify the problems and needs that our product or service addresses.

_____ I maintain ongoing communications with my customers to review plans or to update them on current information or changes.

_____ I remember important dates for my customer and acknowledge them.

_____ I schedule regular meetings or telephone conferences with ongoing customers to assure quality service.

_____ I know and can present the history of my product or service.

_____ I have surveyed the market and I understand the market niche where my product/service will be the most successful.

_____ I know the features of my product/service and can help the customer understand how those features can meet the customers specific needs and expectations.

_____ I understand the environmental trends that will influence the impact of my product/service (e.g., social, technological, economic, and political trends).

_____ I have the authority to solve problems for my customers.

_____ I have access to the resources that will solve problems for my customers.

_____ When my customers have system complaints, I give feedback to the appropriate departments within the system.

_____ **Total Score for Section 3**

INTERPRETATION

The maximum score for any one section is 60 points. The higher your score, the more effective you are in that aspect of customer service. Activities to boost effectiveness in each of these areas can be found in the _Inspiring Fabled Service_ Trainer's Manual.

PARTICIPANT MATERIALS FOR ACTIVITIES

◆ Commitment:

To Make Service Everything Your Company Is and Does

*Communicate everything you can to your associates.
The more they know, the more they care.
Once they care, there is no stopping them.*

Sam Walton

Suggested Reading:

Fabled Service: Ordinary Acts, Extraordinary Outcomes
Chapter 1: The Road to Fabled Service

> Quality service is communicable in two senses: It can be transmitted, and it can be caught. Service that is truly effective in influencing the customers' decisions is fabled service, i.e., service that becomes "fabled" as it is talked about by the customers themselves.

Participant Materials for "Norm's Restaurant" follow on pages 11 to 14.

REFLECTIONS

♦ Fabled service is the only level of service that makes a significant difference to your customers.

♦ Fabled service means customers know why they choose and promote your business passionately.

♦ Fabled service requires a commitment.

♦ Fabled service is an intrinsic value of your business.

♦ Fabled service is based on focused leadership.

♦ The leader's passion for the customer is lived out in broad, clear commitments.

♦ Lived commitments are the footprints that allow others to follow and learn how to create fabled service.

♦ The leader's vision of fabled service should engage the resources and commitments of all constituents.

ACTION STEPS

♦ Commit to leading fabled service that is so meaningful that your customers proclaim it.

♦ Understand that greatness comes in striving toward goals that can never be fully attained.

♦ Envision how great service could be; what currently exists will not engage your people or your customers.

♦ Expect results! Service that doesn't improve your business is not truly service to your customers.

♦ Dream the dream, share the vision, support the effort, and celebrate the results.

NORM'S MENU

- Openness/ Nondefensiveness
- Effective Feedback
- Listening
- Relationship-Building
- "We-Care" Attitude
- You're Important/ No Snubbing Remarks

- Sensitivity
- Open Exchange of Ideas
- Participation
- Experimentation/ Risk Taking
- Responsibility
- Humor
- Confidentially

MENU ITEM CASE STATEMENT

1. The menu item I chose for most effective customer service:

2. My personal reason for choosing this menu item:

3. The reasons why customer service should always include this norm or value:

Menu Observer Sheet

Instructions: Write down your reactions to each presentation as it is performed.

Presentation Item _____
The strengths of the presentation:

The value or norm could be communicated more effectively in the following way(s):

Presentation Item _____
The strengths of the presentation:

The value or norm could be communicated more effectively in the following way(s):

Presentation Item _____
The strengths of the presentation:

The value or norm could be communicated more effectively in the following way(s):

Presentation Item _____
The strengths of the presentation:

The value or norm could be communicated more effectively in the following way(s):

COMMITMENT:

To Be of Service in All That You Do

Excellence is an act won by training and habituation.
We do not act rightly because we have virtue or excellence,
but rather we have those because we have acted rightly.
We are what we repeatedly do.
Excellence then, is not an act, but a habit.

Aristotle

SUGGESTED READING:

Fabled Service: Ordinary Acts, Extraordinary Outcomes
Chapter 2: Fabled Service Is a Way of Life.

> Magic formulas for creating and maintaining quality service do not exist. Service is first and foremost a mind-set, an attitude, a commitment. Service, in short, is not what we do, but who we are. It is a way of living we need to bring to everything we do, if we are to bring it to our customer interactions.

PARTICIPANT MATERIALS FOR "PLANNING TO SERVE" FOLLOW ON PAGES 17 TO 21.

PARTICIPANT MATERIALS FOR "QUALITY CUSTOMER SERVICE"[1] FOLLOW ON PAGES 22 TO 28.

---

[1]Reproduced from *The 1991 Annual: Developing Human Resources* by J.W. Pfeiffer (ed.). Copyright © 1991 by Pfeiffer & Company, San Diego, CA. Used with permission.

REFLECTIONS

♦ Fabled service is a way of life.

♦ Everyday heroes help us believe in our potential to succeed.

♦ Fabled service happens when ordinary people do ordinary things in extraordinary ways.

♦ Your priorities become your people's priorities.

♦ To be excellent, stop doing less-than-excellent things.

♦ People respond to monomaniacs with missions. Share your passion!

♦ Being of service is a process that you will be perfecting the rest of your life.

ACTION STEPS

♦ Be a conscious competent.

♦ Become a student of service. Read and observe all that you can about those who have based their lives on empowering others.

♦ Monitor yourself. Hear what you say. Gauge your responses to employees and customer situations. What do you need to change to practice what you preach?

♦ Work on developing good service habits, one by one. Today, pick the first less-than-excellent thing that you are going to stop doing—and the first excellent thing that you are going to practice. Track your new habits as they develop.

♦ Expect the best of the people you serve, both employees and customers. Provide an environment in which people can excel.

♦ Reward good service in all of your dealings.

♦ Accept the paradox: Being of service is a process that you will be perfecting the rest of your life. At the same time it is a day-in and day-out commitment. Be patient with yourself as the good service habits become ingrained. Do not let lapses become bad habits.

VISIONING THE IDEAL WORK SHEET

Instructions: Write all of the images you saw as the facilitator set the scene for you. Include any vision that will help you to serve your customers more effectively. You have five minutes for this task.

VISIONING THREE FAVORITE IMAGES

Instructions: Record the three images that your subgroup has agreed on from all of your subgroup's responses.

1.

2.

3.

VISIONING INTENTIONAL DIRECTION WORK SHEET

Instructions: With your subgroup, turn the three images that you chose into goal statements. Use an active verb to state the result you want from each of these images. These statements become your intentional direction (i.e., what you intend to accomplish). Following are examples of active verbs:

- ♦ to provide
- ♦ to produce
- ♦ to increase
- ♦ to develop
- ♦ to enhance
- ♦ to communicate
- ♦ to share

GOAL 1

GOAL 2

GOAL 3

When your subgroup has completed this task, choose a spokesperson to report your goals to the entire group.

VISIONING DESIRED OUTCOMES
WORK SHEET

Desired outcomes are the conditions that will exist when the goal has been accomplished. Outcomes can state quantity or quality standards.

Instructions: Choose one of your subgroup's three goals and list it in the space that follows:

GOAL

Finish the following sentence with several specific outcomes you will need to accomplish in order for your goal to become a reality.

This goal will be satisfied when we have:

1.

2.

3.

4.

Post your responses on newsprint and choose a spokesperson to report them to the entire group.

VISIONING ACTION PLAN WORK SHEET

Instructions: With your subgroup, choose one of the desired outcomes you developed. Write it in the space provided.

DESIRED OUTCOME

Fill in the columns that follow with the necessary work steps, resources, accountable people, and time frames.

DESIRED OUTCOME

What work needs to be done to accomplish this outcome?	What resources are needed to accomplish this outcome?	Who will be accountable for assuring that this work is completed?	By what date will this work be completed?
1.	1.	1.	1.
2.	2.	2.	2.
3.	3.	3.	3.
4.	4.	4.	4.

QUALITY WORK SHEET

1a. When I first come in contact with a difficult customer, my usual reaction in terms of thoughts/feelings is...

1b. As a result of my reaction to a difficult customer, my typical behavioral response is...

1c. The consequences of my typical behavioral response are...

2. To form a positive relationship with a difficult customer, I usually...

3. If a difficult customer perceives me as a friend, the consequences are...

4. If a difficult customer perceives me as threatening, the consequences are...

5. The barriers to establishing a positive relationship with a difficult customer and to providing assistance to such a person are...

6. In order to be of assistance to someone, I need to think/feel...

7. The best way to establish a positive relationship with another person is to..

8. The most important thing I have learned about customer service as a result of answering these questions is...

QUALITY DISCUSSION SHEET

1a. What patterns of thoughts/feelings can you identify in people's reactions to difficult customers?

1b. What patterns of behavioral responses can you identify?

1c. What patterns can you identify in the consequences that arise from the behavioral responses?

2. What are the barriers to establishing a positive relationship with a difficult customer?

3. What can be done to build bridges instead of barriers?

4. What generalizations can you draw about forming positive relationships with customers.

5. How can you apply what you have learned about dealing with customers?

QUALITY IDEA SHEET

Providing customers with the service they need and want can be deeply gratifying. No doubt you have experienced the good feeling that comes from helping a customer in just the right way; the customer expresses appreciation by smiling, by complimenting or thanking you, or by returning to your company again for a similar service or product and asking to speak with you. However, we all know that customers can be "difficult," too. A customer whom you perceive as difficult is angry, frustrated, or confused because of an unmet need and expresses that need in an emotional way. It is never pleasant to be faced with behavior that you perceive as difficult; but the experience can be transformed into a positive one that benefits the customer, you, and the company you represent. The following four-step process can be extremely effective in handling a difficult customer:

1. Be aware of your personal perceptions, biases, and reactions. Ask yourself whether you are becoming defensive and annoyed, whether you are breathing more quickly, and whether you are thinking of inappropriate comments to make. An awareness of yourself and your personal reactions allows you to choose consciously to remain calm and to control your own behavior. Your attitude and the thoughts you choose are your most powerful assets in controlling your personal response to any situation.

2. Calm the customer with basic counseling skills. A difficult customer will not behave calmly and rationally until he or she has vented the underlying emotions. Three counseling skills may help you to facilitate this venting and then to establish rapport with the customer:

♦ Maintain a neutral, nondefensive stance. Maintaining neutrality while being verbally attacked is a difficult skill to learn, but it can be managed with practice. The first step is to breathe deeply and slowly from your diaphragm, counting to five as you inhale and again as you exhale. This procedure also allows you enough time to gather your thoughts. Stay focused on the problem presented and not on the person attacking. Difficult customers have a tendency to use "you" statements, placing blame instead of presenting problems realistically. Resisting the impulse to take such comments personally decreases the probability that you will react defensively.

♦ Understand the customer's need by actively listening to his or her concerns. Active listening consists of listening carefully to the customer and then responding by paraphrasing the situation as you understood it. Paraphrasing offers the customer a chance to calm down and realize that he or she was heard accurately. In some cases active listening itself will solve the problem; some customers want only to vent their frustrations and dissatisfaction.

♦ Reflect the customer's feelings by empathizing with the emotion presented. For instance, if the customer is angry, an appropriate response might be "I can understand why you're angry" or "I understand your disappointment." Using "I" messages is a powerful communication technique that allows you to put yourself in the customer's place and understand the emotion expressed as well as the problem involved. When a customer feels personally understood, his or her defensiveness is diminished. Problem analysis and solution are more likely to occur as the result of an objective (detached) approach rather than a subjective (emotionally invested) approach.

3. Diagnose and analyze the situation. Often miscommunication occurs because not enough information has been gathered and analyzed. A good technique for eliciting information from a customer is the use of open questions, which cannot be answered with a simple "yes" or "no"; instead, they encourage lengthy responses. Open questions begin with the words what, when, who, where, which, and how. (A good way to remember them is to think of five W's and an H.) Here are some examples of open questions:

♦ What are your specific concerns?
♦ What information can you share with me so that I can help you?
♦ When did the situation take place?
♦ Which part of the product does not work?
♦ From which department did you purchase the product?
♦ Where did the problem occur?
♦ Who spoke with you?
♦ Who else was present?
♦ What would you like to see happen?
♦ How would you like to resolve this situation?

After you have gathered enough information so that you clearly understand the problem, summarize what you understand the situation to be and confirm with the customer that your understanding is correct.

Work with the customer to develop an action plan for solving the identified problem. Help the customer to understand the alternatives that are open to him or her as well as the consequences of each alternative. Clearly communicate company policies and/or any constraints that apply. State positively what will be done to solve the customer's problem and when the action will take place; explain the specific procedure that will be used to follow through on the service promised.[2]

Finally, thank the customer for the valuable feedback given to your company and encourage the continuation of open communication.

---

[2]Although this approach may not be consistent with standard practice in the past, it is consistent with the current drive toward empowerment in organizations. "Empowered" employees are ones who, within the realm of their own jobs, seize opportunities, make decisions, and solve problems on their own (to the greatest extent possible and with the encouragement of management).

COMMITMENT:

To Act on the Belief That You Are in Business to Serve Customers

Perhaps the cardinal rule of customer service is:
Know thy customer!
Karl Albrecht

SUGGESTED READING:

Fabled Service: Ordinary Acts, Extraordinary Outcomes
Chapter 3: Fabled Service Is Defined by the Customer

> Customers assess the service quality of a company by evaluating the caliber of the service they receive from the perspective of the service they desire. Theirs is the only definition that counts. Providing service requires careful attention to the changing needs and desires of the customers, making them the drivers of your business.

PARTICIPANT MATERIALS FOR "CUSTOMER SERVICE BASEBALL" FOLLOW ON PAGES 31 TO 35.

PARTICIPANT MATERIALS FOR "1-800-SERVICE" FOLLOW ON PAGES 36 TO 38.

REFLECTIONS

♦ If the customer doesn't care about it, it is not service.

♦ The foundation of legendary service is to believe that you are in business to serve the customer and then to act accordingly.

♦ In order to serve your customers, you must understand their values and consider how you are uniquely positioned to meet their needs.

♦ Every interaction your customers have with any aspect of your business creates a "Moment of Truth" in which they judge your commitment to their service—and make the decision whether or not to return.

♦ The best use of your time is being actively and responsively involved with your customers.

♦ Meeting expectations is required to be tolerated. Exceeding expectations is required to be fabled.

♦ Unexpected. Undeserved. Unnecessary. Service that makes the difference is in the margins.

♦ The only difference among companies is in how we treat our customers.

ACTION STEPS

♦ Question all of your business precepts. Weigh what you do against what your customers say you should do. Now.

♦ Develop a simple system to elicit constant feedback.

♦ Involve front-line employees in information gathering.

♦ Ask open-ended questions; accept responses seriously—and gratefully.

♦ Incorporate what you learn from customers into strategies.

♦ Respond personally to all suggestions and criticisms.

♦ Underpromise and overdeliver.

♦ Keep decision making as close to the customer as possible.

♦ Analyze business from your customers' perspective: Use your products and services; visit your locations.

♦ Commit to continuous improvement. Always surpass your best performance, as each experience sets a new benchmark for the customer.

BASEBALL TEAM ONE TASK SHEET

Instructions: Your team has the responsibility to get the whole team to second base. No one can win unless everyone wins. Each base is a key process in winning the game.

Your team has twenty (20) minutes to develop a vision of customer satisfaction. You have all been customers. What do you want and need when you are a customer? What are your expectations? To get to second base, you must do the following tasks and record your progress on newsprint:

1. What are basic qualities of customer satisfaction? See a vision and write it down or draw it.

2. List two (2) ways to find out the needs of customers.

3. Create a model on newsprint that represents a customer needs assessment.

BASEBALL TEAM TWO TASK SHEET

Instructions: Your team has the responsibility to get the whole team to third base. No one can win unless everyone wins. Each base is a key process in winning the game.

Your team has twenty (20) minutes to develop five long-range goals that will give definitive direction to meeting the needs of the customers on first base. What do you intend to do to ensure customer satisfaction? Write five long-range goals that will meet customer needs and assure quality service to customers. Begin each goals with an action verb, such as "provide," "enhance," "promote," or "increase." Record your goals on newsprint.

1.

2.

3.

4.

5.

BASEBALL TEAM THREE TASK SHEET

Instructions: Your team has the responsibility to get the whole team to home plate. No one can win unless everyone wins. Each base is a key process in winning the game.

Your team has twenty (20) minutes to write an action plan to achieve each of the goals created by Team Two. Write three (3) action steps for each goal. What specific work has to be done to accomplish the goals, and what resources must be found to apply the action?

GOAL # 1

1.

2.

3.

GOAL # 2

1.

2.

3.

GOAL # 3

1.

2.

3.

GOAL # 4

1.

2.

3.

GOAL # 5

1.

2.

3.

BASEBALL OBSERVER SHEET

Instructions: Your role is to observe both the process and the content developed by the teams around the table. Process reflects how the group works together, and content involves the product the group produces.

When the facilitator asks for your comments or suggestions, respond in the following manner:

1. I wish to make a comment or suggestion about:

   _____ Understanding customer needs and satisfaction

   _____ Setting long-range goals for customer service and customer satisfaction

   _____ Developing action steps and identifying resources to achieve goals

2. I wish to make a comment about the group process (focus on behaviors and attitudes that helped or hindered the process):

1-800-Service Idea Sheet

Instructions: Write about the situation that you visualized. Be specific about the customer service response you received. Was it positive or negative? What did you like? What did you dislike? You have three minutes to write about your experience.

1-800-Service Work Sheet

Instructions: Using the letters in the word SERVICE, write attitudinal, behavioral, or action responses to your partner's situation. What are the most appropriate customer service responses (e.g., Sensitivity, Experience, Respect, etc.). You will have ten minutes to be as creative as possible.

S

E

R

V

I

C

E

1-800-SERVICE RESPONSES

Instructions: Write down five quality responses that you could use to respond to the customer situations you heard about in your subgroup. You will have five minutes.

1.

2.

3.

4.

5.

 # COMMITMENT:

To Serve Those Who Serve the Customer

What transforms slave-like labor into exalted service are the amount of skills required to provide it; the importance of the need to desire served; the relationship between the server and the served; and prevailing religious, moral, and social opinion.

Russell L. Ackoff

SUGGESTED READING:

Fabled Service: Ordinary Acts, Extraordinary Outcomes
Chapter 4: Fabled Service Is Everyone's Job

> Service leadership starts at the top of the company, or it doesn't start at all. In every organization dealing with the public, there are only two job descriptions: everybody either directly support the customers or supports the people who do. Service then is a continuum, with everyone being focused ultimately on assuring customer care.

PARTICIPANT MATERIALS FOR "C-SCALE PROBLEM SOLVING" FOLLOW ON PAGES 41 TO 43.

PARTICIPANT MATERIALS FOR "TEMPERAMENT TENNIS" FOLLOW ON PAGES 44 TO 52.

REFLECTIONS

♦ If service at your company is to be legendary, it must be everybody's business.

♦ There are two job descriptions: Those who take care of customers and those who take care of caretakers.

♦ Your expectations of the people who serve the customer: Good judgment, positive attitude, passion for the customer, desire to be part of a winning team, willingness to give their all.

♦ Your people's expectations of you: All of the above, plus meaningful work, respect, the opportunity to share the big picture, a clear set of standards, ongoing training, appreciation and recognition, responsibility for decisions, freedom and support to be their best.

ACTION STEPS

♦ Ask yourself how you can better serve the needs of your direct customers, so that they can do the same for their customers.

♦ Make certain there are no jobs labeled "Customer Service." Service is everyone's job.

♦ Get to know the people at all levels of your company—and allow them to get to know you.

♦ Be alert to what makes you a happy customer, then apply what you learn to your company.

♦ Equip your people to deliver fabled service: Share the vision, train them in the basics, provide them with all of the necessary tools, give them feedback, get out of their way.

C-SCALE NOTES

C = Consider the customer's problem or complaint. Listen actively and paraphrase what you understand the problem to be. Reach agreement that you understand the problem as presented.

D = Develop a problem definition or goal with the customer. Phrase it as a question: How can we...? Write the question on newsprint.

E = Examine the problem with analysis, and gather information about the problem. Ask the customer to tell you what obstacles stand in the way of solving the problem. Check your assumptions, and look at the problem from many perspectives.

F = Find out the answers to the basic questions: Who? What? Where? When? Why? Listen actively.

G = Generate as many alternatives as possible. Keep asking the question, "How can we...?" Write all of the alternatives on newsprint.

A = Assess the alternatives by working with the customer to develop the qualities necessary for an effective solution. These criteria will help you to choose the most feasible alternative from the list. Ask the following question: "What qualities or standards would the best solution to this problem have?"

B = Build credibility by evaluating the effectiveness of the chosen alternative. Reassess or revise as needed. If we use this solution, what will be the outcome? Implement the solution and evaluate results.

C = Create a new vision for a problem-free relationship. What does it look, sound, and feel like? You are ready to face new problems as they arise. Celebrate!

C-SCALE ROLE PLAY QUESTIONS

1. What can you tell me about the problem you are experiencing?

2. May I see if I understand what you have told me?

3. How can we phrase your problem in the form of a question so we can develop some alternative solutions?

4. What are the major obstacles to solving the problem?

5. Will you help me to understand the basics? Who is involved? What happened? Where did it occur? When did you first notice the problem? Why do you think the problem happened?

6. Will you help me to generate some possible solutions? Let's be as creative as possible in thinking of answers to this problem, so we won't evaluate the solutions just yet.

7. What qualities or standards would the best alternative have? Will you help me to develop those criteria?

8. If we choose an alternative based on our criteria, how will we know if the solution has worked?

9. Will you contact me after you have implemented this alternative and let me know how it went?

10. What kind of working relationship should we envision? What would it look, sound, or feel like? Can we agree to that kind of a working relationship in the future? How shall we celebrate?

C-Scale (Customer Scale)

C = Conscious

U = Understood

S = Satisfied

T = Trusted

O = Oriented

M = Mellowed

E = Energized

R = Returning to you for products and services

TEMPERAMENT TYPES[3]

ARTISAN PERSONALITY	GUARDIAN PERSONALITY
◆ Is action oriented ◆ Takes bold and impressive actions ◆ Thrives on following impulses ◆ Lives in the moment, takes risks, loves adventure	◆ Is accountable ◆ Does duty unselfishly and responsibly ◆ Maintains traditions and institutions of society loyally ◆ Participates actively in service clubs
RATIONAL PERSONALITY	**IDEALIST PERSONALITY**
◆ Is competent ◆ Uses precision in thought and language ◆ Deals with theoretical complexity and designs abstract models ◆ Uses strategic ability for long-range planning	◆ Is relationship oriented ◆ Strives to be authentic ◆ Has rapport with others and inspires others to develop full potential ◆ Catalyzes groups and helps others to grow

[3]See *Survival Games Personalities Play,* by Eve Delunas, 1992, Carmel, CA: Sunflower Ink. Used with permission.

THE GUARDIAN TEMPERAMENT

Instructions: Please brainstorm with your subgroup to answer the questions that follow. The values and behaviors you decide on will be used as your strategies to win the tennis game.

What four values are most important to this temperament type?

1.

2.

3.

4.

List eight behaviors, both negative and positive, that this temperament type uses on a regular basis when interacting with others.

1.

2.

3.

4.

5.

6.

7.

8.

THE ARTISAN TEMPERAMENT

Instructions: Please brainstorm with your subgroup to answer the questions that follow. The values and behaviors you decide on will be used as your strategies to win the tennis game.

What four values are most important to this temperament type?

1.

2.

3.

4.

List eight behaviors, both negative and positive, that this temperament type uses on a regular basis when interacting with others.

1.

2.

3.

4.

5.

6.

7.

8.

THE IDEALIST TEMPERAMENT

Instructions: Please brainstorm with your subgroup to answer the questions that follow. The values and behaviors you decide on will be used as your strategies to win the tennis game.

What four values are most important to this temperament type?

1.

2.

3.

4.

List eight behaviors, both negative and positive, that this temperament type uses on a regular basis when interacting with others.

1.

2.

3.

4.

5.

6.

7.

8.

THE RATIONAL TEMPERAMENT

Instructions: Please brainstorm with your subgroup to answer the questions that follow. The values and behaviors you decide on will be used as your strategies to win the tennis game.

What four values are most important to this temperament type?

1.

2.

3.

4.

List eight behaviors, both negative and positive, that this temperament type uses on a regular basis when interacting with others.

1.

2.

3.

4.

5.

6.

7.

8.

TEMPERAMENT TENNIS COURT SET-UP

GUARDIANS need to:	RATIONALS need to:
♦ Belong ♦ Do their duty ♦ Be responsible **Team 3**	♦ Achieve ♦ Exercise their ingenuity ♦ Demonstrate competence **Team 4**
ARTISANS need to:	IDEALISTS need to:
♦ Be free to follow their impulses ♦ Demonstrate skillfulness ♦ Make an impression **Team 2**	♦ Become self-actualized ♦ Develop potential in self and others ♦ Be authentic **Team 1**

TEMPERAMENT TENNIS RULES

Instructions: All values and behaviors used in the game are related to customer service. The values and behaviors that your subgroup generated are the strategies you will use to win the game.

The game consists of four points. The team that receives four points first, wins the round. A tie-breaker point is served if the score becomes 3 to 3, meaning that the next point determines the winner.

Team 1 begins by serving a value or a behavior to Team 3. Team 3 may accept the value or behavior as something it would like and admire as a customer or reject the value or behavior as something that would irritate or frustrate the team as a customer. The receiving team has two minutes to discuss the decision and offers two sentences to share the rationale for the decision.

If a team accepts a value or behavior, the serving team receives one point. If a team rejects a value or behavior, the receiving team wins the point.

Team 1 alternates, just as in the game of tennis, by serving one point to Team 3 and one point to Team 4 until the round is completed.

Example: Idealists serve one value or behavior to Guardians, who may accept or reject it. Idealists then serve one value or behavior to the Rationals, who may accept or reject. Idealists alternate serving to Guardians and Rationals until the game is won.

Round One: Idealists serve to Guardians and Rationals.

Round Two: Rationals serve to Artisans and Guardians.

Round Three: Guardians serve Idealists and Artisans.

Round Four: Artisans serve to Rationals and Idealists.

TEMPERAMENT TENNIS
OBSERVER SHEET

Which temperament type is serving?

Which temperament types are receiving?

Which values and behaviors are accepted by which temperament types?

Which values and behaviors are rejected by which temperament types?

What trends do you notice in what is being accepted and rejected by each of the receiving temperament types?

COMMITMENT:

To Design Every Part of Your Business With Service As the Desired Outcome

At the core of every great customer service organization is a package of systems and a training program to inculcate those programs into the soul of that company.

Ken Blanchard and Sheldon Bowers

SUGGESTED READING:

Fabled Service: Ordinary Acts, Extraordinary Outcomes
Chapter 5: Fabled Service Is Designed Into the System

> Each interaction gives a customer a definite impression of the company's commitment to service. Therefore, all systems design should be concerned with how to best support and enhance individual interactions with customers. The fewer the systems, the better; all should be designed to maximize decision making as close to the customer as possible.

PARTICIPANT MATERIALS FOR "HIRE RIGHT" FOLLOW ON PAGES 55 TO 56.

PARTICIPANT MATERIALS FOR "NEEDS, FEATURES, AND BENEFITS"[4] FOLLOW ON PAGES 57 TO 60.

REFLECTIONS

- ◆ People's performance from company to company has more to do with the quality of the management than the innate quality of the people themselves.

- ◆ The front line can't lie: The superstructure reveals the infrastructure.

- ◆ To thrill to the care of your customers means to have what they want when they want it.

- ◆ Design service into the system from the start.

- ◆ The hallmarks of systems that support service are simplicity and relevance.

- ◆ Service becomes systemic when designed into the organization's structure, processes, goals, expectations, and work environment.

ACTION STEPS

- ◆ Redesign your organizational structure to reflect your commitment to the customer. Involve all constituents in the process.

- ◆ Collaborate on the vision and mission of the company. Strategies and goals should be consistent with the reason you are in business.

- ◆ Test strategies, products, and processes against customer perceptions before implementing.

- ◆ Always ask: "How can we do this better?" Then listen to the answers.

- ◆ Establish an ongoing forum for your employees to communicate what works and what does not.

- ◆ Eradicate red tape—with a vengeance!

RIGHT/WRONG ATTITUDES

Right Attitudes for Serving Customers

Wrong Attitudes for Serving Customers

JOB DESCRIPTION WORK SHEET

Instructions: Please identify four (4) standards or criteria that should be part of any job description in an organizaion that values service.

1.

2.

3.

4.

NEEDS, FEATURES, AND BENEFITS THEORY SHEET

In work and other aspects of life, we all find occasions when we are trying to "sell" something to another person. One may be actually trying to sell a product or service to a potential buyer. One may be "selling" a vision or concept while trying to solicit a donation or support for a worthy cause. Or one may be trying to satisfy a dissatisfied person by "selling" him or her a solution, for example, trying to "sell" an employee the benefits of a job change or trying to "sell" a family member a change of vacation plans. Thus, everyone engages in some type of customer service. Whether or not the customer is being asked to exchange monetary resources for a product or service, good customer service means that the customer winds up being happy with the interaction he or she has had.

The most important concepts to understand in order to help the customer to be satisfied with the exchange are as follows:

- ◆ The customer's needs;
- ◆ The benefits the customer will receive as a result of the exchange (for example, purchasing the product or service);
- ◆ The features of the proposed solution/product or service that make it attractive to the customer; and
- ◆ How those features provide benefits to the customer and meet the customer's needs.

A salesperson sells either a product or a service. In order to be successful, the salesperson has several obligations. The most important obligation is to become so familiar with the product or service that it becomes internalized as something familiar and something that the salesperson values a great deal. Without this understanding and sense of importance of the product or service, the salesperson has little chance of convincing anyone that the product or service has value and will satisfy customer needs. Thus, the first and most important obligation is to understand the case for the product or service. The case is all of the reasons that anyone would want to buy the product or service.

Consider the case of a consultant who is offering training services. In order to be successful, the consultant must become so familiar with the services offered that they become internalized as something of value. Without this understanding and sense of importance, the consultant has little chance of convincing anyone that the services have value and will satisfy customer needs.

NEEDS

If a person values something, it is easy to talk about it. However, a more important skill is getting someone else to talk about why he or she needs or would value the product or service and actively listening to what the person says. The best way to find out about the customer's needs is to ask the customer. A salesperson must know how to design open-ended questions to find out what the customer needs and then must actively listen by paraphrasing the answers heard so that the customer knows that he or she is understood. A good salesperson may spend 80 percent of his or her time eliciting and listening to the customer's needs and communicating his or her understanding of those needs by paraphrasing what the customer has just said.

The salesperson's skill in listening for the customer's needs enables him or her to sell the case so that the case matches the needs of the customer. This is where it is essential for the salesperson to know the product or service well, to value it enough that his or her genuine enthusiasm for it is evident, and to quickly adjust the discussion of features and benefits to match the customer's needs.

In the case of the consultant who is offering training services, an opening question might be to ask, "What is the problem that you want to solve?" If the answer to the question is that supervisors need to learn delegation skills, an active-listening response might be to ask, "Your supervisors don't have time to plan and coordinate because they end up doing the tasks themselves?" If this indeed is the case, the consultant would sell the features of a supervisory training program that are relevant to delegation.

FEATURES

Assuming that the enthusiasm and value for the product or service exist, the salesperson also must have information about the product or service. First, the salesperson must fully understand the product or service: What are the features of the product or service that make it valuable? What does it offer that is unique? What makes it different from other products or services that are available to the customer? This may require researching the product or service to find-out its history, its purpose, why it is valuable, and how it will benefit the customer. This is learning the features of the product or service. These features must not only be known but also believed by the salesperson, so that when he or she speaks about the product or service, enthusiasm for the features is evident in his or her voice, body language, and whole personality.

The consultant who is selling training services might communicate that his or her training program features teaching an understanding of the supervisory position in the organization and teaching the skills of delegating, planning, and so on. The program may be unique in that it includes role playing. It may differ from other services that are available in that it includes videotaped modeling and writing in journals.

The process of selling is the same no matter what is sold. The ingredient that sets a successful salesperson apart from others is the innate enthusiasm and value the salesperson holds for the product or service. The axiom is "Sell something you value or find a way to value what you sell." The value is contained in the features.

BENEFITS

The next step is for the salesperson to communicate the value to the customer. This cannot be done in a believable way unless the salesperson takes the time to find out the customer's needs and how the product or service can benefit the customer, that is, meet the customer's needs. Only then can the salesperson tell how the features of the product or service will benefit the customer or satisfy the customer's needs. For the consultant who is selling training services, a benefit may be to increase a unit's productivity or to reduce the supervisors' overtime.

SUMMARY

In summary, presenting a case involves finding value for a product or service and learning about it so well that enthusiasm is a natural part of speaking about it. The next step is listening to the customer to discover his or her needs. Third, one must let the customer know how the features of the product or service will benefit the customer better than those of other available products or services. This is accomplished by emphasizing how the customer's needs will be met.

Although the final step is closing, it is not as proactive as the preceding ones. It is important to let the customer make up his or her own mind. The foregoing process should be sufficient to ensure a positive closure.

NEEDS, FEATURES, AND BENEFITS WORK SHEET

Instructions: Please answer each of the following questions when you are instructed to do so.

1. Write down the name of your hobby or activity. Write one sentence about how you became interested in it.

2. Why is there a need for this hobby or activity? Who needs it? (Please answer in one sentence.)

3. What is a feature of this hobby or activity (something inherent that it offers to someone)? (Please answer in one sentence.)

4. What benefit will someone receive from this hobby or activity? (Please answer in one sentence.)

5. Convince someone to join you in this hobby or activity. (Please write one sentence.)

COMMITMENT:

To Be in Business to Serve Society

To give real service, you must add something which cannot be bought or measured with money, and that is sincerity and integrity.
Donald A. Adams

SUGGESTED READING:

Fabled Service: Ordinary Acts, Extraordinary Outcomes
Chapter 6: Fabled Service Is Inseparable From Integrity

> Quality service is realizable only in an organizational culture that values integrity. The company must exhibit a win-win attitude. Companies that operate with integrity are focused on fairness as an underlying principle, fairness for all constituencies at all times.

PARTICIPANT MATERIALS FOR "SERVICE INTEGRITY" FOLLOW ON PAGES 63 TO 67.

REFLECTIONS

♦ Experience and history show that you can lead service excellence only if you value integrity.

♦ Consider these words from two cultures vastly separated by time, geography, and technology:

Wealth does not bring goodness, but goodness wealth and every other blessing, both to the individual and the state.

Socrates, 469-399 B.C.

We are not in business to make maximum profit for our shareholders. We are in business for only one reason—to serve society. If business does not serve society, society will not long tolerate our profits, not even our existence.

Kenneth Dayton, restating Socrates, A.D. 1975

ACTION STEPS

♦ Where there is dissonance between your company's principles and your personal principles, align with the higher value.

♦ Communicate your standards clearly, both in word and deed.

♦ Insist on adherence to standards; it is imperative for success at your company.

♦ Trust your instincts. You will feel balanced when you operate with integrity.

♦ Have your heart in your work and your work in your heart.

FACTS ABOUT HORSE RACING

Horse races have been held since ancient times. In the United States, more people attend horse races than any other type of sporting event.

Jockeys control the horses in a race. The skill of the jockey in handling the horse can determine whether or not the horse wins the race. Jockeys wear special jackets and caps, which are called "silks." The color and style of the silks identifies the owner of the horse.

One of the features of horse racing is the chance to win money by betting on horses to finish first, second, and third in a race. The owners of the horses that finish in the top three places win prize money, known as a "purse." "Racing forms" are used at race tracks to give information to spectators about the race horses. Each horse has a record consisting of how it has performed in previous races. People wager billions of dollars on horse races yearly.

HORSES IN THE RACE

- ◆ Authenticity

- ◆ Focus

- ◆ Consistency

- ◆ Value

- ◆ Honesty

- ◆ Ethics

- ◆ Completeness

- ◆ Purpose

RACE HORSE OWNER:
QUICK WRITE

Horse's Name_____

Instructions: Please take five (5) minutes to write down your reasons for buying this horse. When you think about this horse, what do you see, hear, and feel?

RACE HORSE JOCKEY:
QUICK WRITE

Horse's Name_____

Instructions: Please take five (5) minutes to write down all of the reasons you like to ride this horse. How will your horse reach the finish line first? What are your horse's finest qualities?

RACING FORM

Horse's Name_____

Instructions: You will use this form to present information about your horse to the Press Club. Combine the Race Horse Owner information and the Race Horse Jockey information to convince the Press Club to feature your horse in the next edition.

1. What has made your horse a winner in the past?

2. List the feature and qualities that will enable your horse to win this race.

3. What are the benefits that your horse brings to this race?

4. Prepare a five-minute presentation to give at the Press Club. Record this information on newsprint, and use it as a visual aid to enhance your presentation.

# COMMITMENT:

To Create and Sustain the Vision

The first responsibility of a leader is to define reality.
The last is to say thank you. In between the two, the leaders
must become a servant and a debtor.
That sums up the progress of an artful leader.

Max DePree

SUGGESTED READING:

Fabled Service: Ordinary Acts, Extraordinary Outcomes
Chapter 7: Fabled Service Is Empowered by Leadership

> Only genuine leadership at every level of the company can
> provide the inspiration necessary to sustain committed ser-
> vice on the part of all employees. The principle tool of service
> leadership is communication. To begin with, the service
> leader has to champion quality at all times, modeling, coach-
> ing, and reinforcing good service at every opportunity.

PARTICIPANT MATERIALS FOR "YOUR LEADERSHIP ROLE" FOLLOW ON PAGES 71 TO 73.

PARTICIPANT MATERIALS FOR "REFLECTION AND ACTION" FOLLOW ON PAGES 74 TO 75.

REFLECTIONS

♦ Fabled service leaders master how to work with their people to create the customer-serving vision.

♦ The urge to serve others is the defining element of service leadership.

♦ The key to fabled service leadership is making the commitment to act on your knowledge and beliefs.

ACTION STEPS

♦ Work with people to set and achieve high goals and exceed personal expectations.

♦ Delegate authority and responsibility.

♦ Clear hurdles to success.

♦ Encourage risk taking.

♦ Provide all tools necessary for success.

♦ Motivate through inspiring vision.

♦ See the best in and expect the best from everyone.

♦ Recognize accomplishments; show appreciation.

HERSEY/BLANCHARD LEADERSHIP DEFINITIONS[5]

Leadership is the outcome of certain behaviors demonstrated by a person to influence or motivate people to perform tasks.

Circle the one word in this definition that you feel is most important in terms of leadership.

---

[5]See *Management of Organizational Behavior: Utilizing Human Resources,* by Paul Hersey and Kenneth H. Blanchard, 1982, Englewood Cliffs, NJ: Prentice Hall.

DIRECTIVE/SUPPORTIVE LEADERSHIP SHEET

Please complete the columns with examples of specific behaviors that demonstrate a positive response to customers and that will influence and motivate customers.

Directive Behaviors	Supportive Behaviors

Ideal Customer Service
Leader Sheet

Use the knowledge you have gained about customer service leadership to write, draw a picture, or compose a poem that will communicate what you have learned.

Please share your information with your subgroup when requested to do so.

REFLECTION SHEET

♦ What have I learned about myself and my leadership role when I serve customers?

♦ What have I learned about planning when I serve my customers?

♦ What have I learned about the training competencies and training others in customer service?

♦ What have I learned about understanding my product or service and how I can use that knowledge in serving customers?

PRESENTATION RESOURCE SHEET

Every presentation needs to be organized with an opening, a body, and a conclusion. The opening accounts for 10 percent of the presentation time, the body for 80 percent, and the conclusion for 10 percent.

THE OPENING: "TELL THEM WHAT YOU'LL TELL THEM"

The opening consists of two components: a "hook" (question, statistic, story, skit, role play, group sharing, or example) that captures the audience's attention and a review of the plan for the presentation. This stage should meet the audience's needs for safety and belonging.

THE BODY: "TELL THEM"

The body should have no more than three to five main ideas, and each idea should be supported with information or examples. It is useful to vary the instructional strategies for the ideas. If you present one idea in a didactic fashion, then you might want to use a skit, a role play, and a group discussion to convey subsequent points. This stage should meet the audience's needs for self-esteem and self-actualization.

THE CONCLUSION: "TELL THEM WHAT YOU TOLD THEM"

In the conclusion you summarize the objective and the main ideas that you presented; review action plans and encourage follow through, and answer questions. This stage should meet the audience's needs for self-actualization.